Ac

Writing Better Action Using Cinematic Techniques

IAN THOMAS HEALY

Local Hero Press

http://localheropress.ianthealy.com

Cover and book design by Ian Thomas Healy

ISBN: 0615637981
ISBN-13: 978-0615637983

Printed in the United States of America

First Printing May 2012

For Allison

CONTENTS

Introduction	i
Part I: Defining the Action Scene	7
Part II: Building Blocks of Action Scenes	12
Part III: Types of Action Scenes	26
Part IV: Gratuitous Explosions and Other Action Downfalls	38
Part V: Putting It All Together	41
Part VI: Tips and Tricks	46
Glossary	49

INTRODUCTION

Excerpt from Pariah's Moon by Ian Thomas Healy, Copyright 2011

He heard a rustle and footsteps behind him and turned to see three men—two Elves and a Dwarf with an eye patch—had entered the store. One Elf and the Dwarf split up and headed toward different aisles. Giele's hackles raised; he knew a flanking maneuver when he saw it. The third man, tall and broad-shouldered, ducked to avoid a low-hanging collection of lanterns and smiled without humor at Cianid. He wore a hat with a shallow brim and a quail feather stuck in the band. His blond hair fell about his shoulders, framing a handsome face that spoke of good breeding. Over a blue silk shirt, his soft leather vest had been dyed black but for the decorative fringe work, which was the color of dried blood. He rolled a match back and forth in his teeth and walked with a bully's swagger.

In spite of the heat of the day, he sported a long, dark coat.

He wore a single pistol on a belt across his waist, riding high for what must have been a cross-body draw. The pistol's grip was well-polished and the edges of the holster were scuffed from use.

"Howdy, Cianid. You havin' trouble with this stranger?" He ducked to avoid a low-hanging collection of lanterns and smiled without a trace of humor. His drawl was much stronger than most of those Giele had heard so far in Verigo.

A muscle twitched in Cianid's jaw. She had history with this man, and not of a pleasant sort, from what Giele could infer. "He's just a customer, Rarik."

Rarik. So this was the man who'd been so free with his knife upon Shali. The slow burn of righteous fury started to spread outward from Giele's heart to the tips of his fingers and toes.

Rarik plucked an apple from a bin and polished it on the sleeve of his blue silk shirt. "And so am I. How much?" He jingled his purse as he took a bite.

The other Elf and Dwarf had moved into positions where they could attack Giele without being caught in each other's crossfire if they chose to do so. They all wore pistols, but Giele's was in one of his saddlebags, and his bow in its case outside with his horse. All he had on him was the knife given to him by the 136th. He winced at the irony. They often joked in the Army about the futility of bringing a sword to an archery battle, and here he had brought a knife to a gunfight.

"On the house, Rarik." Cianid's clenched jaw stood out in sharp relief.

His eyes widened in mock surprise. "Oh ho, so you're giving things away, are you?" He stepped toward her. "What else is free today?"

"Easy, Scarface." The Dwarf cocked his pistol and pointed it at Giele when he started to move. Giele never even saw him draw it. "This ain't none of your business."

Cianid stood her ground as Rarik circled her, looking her up and down in appreciation. His eyes lingered upon her like a hungry cat regarding a pigeon. "I've told you before and I'll tell you again. No."

"Come on, little filly. I ain't gonna hurt you. I just thought maybe we could get to know each other a little better is all." He took another bite of apple and wiped juice from his chin with the back of his hand.

"I'm not one of your whores." She put on a brave face but the quiver in her voice betrayed her fear of him. Giele shifted his weight onto the balls of his feet.

He stopped behind her. She stiffened as he leaned forward to speak into her ear. "Ah, but you should be, with a face and a body like yours. You could be one of my high-priced attractions. Don't you agree, boys? Wouldn't you pay real crowns for a piece of this ass?" He slapped her rear and she jumped away as if scalded by his touch.

The other two thugs murmured their agreement. Giele's fingers found the iron handle of the heavy cooking pan where it rested amid his pile of supplies—a poor weapon, but better than nothing. He hadn't moved his hand more than an inch since the men first entered the store. He moved it another inch.

"Get out of my store, Rarik. I want no part of your business."

"But I want part of yours." He leered at her and licked his lips. "And I always get what I want."

"The lady asked you to leave, friend," said Giele. "Perhaps it would be best if you did."

Rarik spun to face him and took another bite of apple. He chewed for a moment and then spat it back in Giele's face. "You're that feller everyone's raisin' a stink about. The marked man. I already done threw you out of my place today. I'd be doin' this town a favor if I shot you where you stand."

Giele made no move to wipe the fragments of apple from his face, but tightened his grip on the iron handle. "Seems rather like I could say the same thing about you." He kept his voice low.

"What was that? What did you say, you boar-rutting moon-faced son of a diseased whore?"

He took one more step toward Giele, and that was close enough.

We all know what's going to happen next; we've all seen this scene, or a variation of it, played in dozens of different movies. Most writers, though, get all skittish and twitchy at the idea of writing something as complicated as a fight in a general store. How many times have you found yourself facing an incipient action scene with trepidation? Maybe you wrote a couple lines, then quit. Or maybe you skipped ahead. Or maybe you just knocked your hero on the head so you wouldn't have to write it.

The fear of action scenes is all too common among writers today, and in this book, I'll give you the tools to overcome that fear. Instead of fearing your action scenes, you'll look forward to them with all the anticipation of a kid on Halloween afternoon. But first, let's look at how we got here in the first place—why action scenes are the bane of so many writers.

IT'S HOLLYWOOD'S FAULT, OR, WHY JOHNNY CAN'T WRITE ACTION SCENES

I'm going to go out on a limb here and assume everyone reading this has seen a movie. If you've never seen a movie, well, you probably shouldn't be reading this book because you have a barn to raise and a beard to grow.

In the 19th Century and before, writers had far more leeway to write action than they do today. Outside of live performances, books were the only game in town when it came to entertaining people. Consequently, readers had to imagine whatever the writer described, sometimes without any frame of reference at all. Motion pictures changed all that. Suddenly, filmmakers could take their imagination and, through the use of carefully-planned stunts and special effects, film exactly what *they* were imagining. By committing those images to film, they shared their action scenes as they intended them to look with mass audiences. Instead of audiences having to imagine, they could sit passively and observe someone else's imagination.

For example: *The two men, one garbed in shining black and the other in soft brown, battled across the floor with their laser swords.* I'll bet most of you immediately pictured the Darth Vader-Obi-Wan Kenobi duel in *Star Wars: A New Hope.* Your memory of the scene as it was shot filled in the details without me describing them. If I'd written that sentence as part of a story that involved neither of those characters, you'd still think of the movie scene, because that's how motion pictures have affected the modern reader—by giving us a common frame of reference. For a century now, from the earliest silent films loaded with dangerous and creative stunts, to the shootouts of the Westerns, to the car chases of the '60s and '70s, through the martial arts movie craze of the '80s and the CGI era after that, action scenes have become indelibly imprinting upon our minds. We've become a visually-oriented culture instead of an imagination-oriented one.

So what's a modern writer to do to reach this jaded reading audience?

DIRECTING THE SCENE

To effectively create an action scene that meets both the needs of the story and the needs of the reader, you must think more like a movie director. This means that you must consider not only the characters and their goals, but their *motion* through a given scene. Action scenes require characters to be in motion, and the effective description of that motion is what makes the difference between a good, cinematic-quality action scene and a merely adequate one. By making this transition from good to great, your action scenes will be exciting to read, memorable, and have a visceral quality that will have your readers turning the pages, desperate to keep up.

Blocking and staging are terms for the motions a character performs during the course of the scene and in what order. Example: Joe enters the room, spots his opponent, Bob, and charges to attack him at the room's center. Those are three simple stage directions one might find in a script, but they're just as effective to use when planning out an action scene in a novel.

Scripting is the dialogue of the characters uttered during an action scene. It's neither necessary nor welcome to place every single shout, grunt, or groan inside quotation marks. This is, after all, an action scene. But in movies, characters always seem to find enough time to carry on some kind of conversation during action scenes, whether taunting their opponents, arguing with them, calling for help, or uttering pithy zingers. Depending upon the tone you're trying to create, dialogue can be a good addition to any action scene that demands cinematic quality.

Choreographing is the planning of specific stunts performed by the characters in your scene. Choreographing is not the same thing as blocking. In the above example, the blocking of Joe is to enter the room and move to meet Bob. Once they're engaged in actual combat, choreographing takes the place of blocking. If Joe swings with a heavy left hook and follows it up with a knee to the nuts, that's choreographing. In other words, choreographing is the blow-by-blow breakdown of any given action scene, the interaction of characters.

Taking the example of Joe vs. Bob a little further, we can identify the characteristics of each part of the scene:

> Joe flung open the door *[Blocking]*. Bob smirked at him from across the room, raised his hand, and beckoned to Joe *[Blocking]*. "Come get some," he said *[Scripting]*.
>
> With an inarticulate yell of rage, Joe charged across the floor as Bob dropped into a fighting stance *[Blocking]*. Joe launched a heavy left hook at Bob, but the man ducked underneath the blow *[Choreographing]*. Before Bob could respond, Joe drove his knee hard in between Bob's legs *[Choreographing]*.

> Bob turned the same color as the floor, grabbed himself, and collapsed *[Blocking]*.

Poor Bob. If only he knew the fundamentals of action scenes, he might have given a better accounting of himself. Let's see if we can teach him.

PART I: DEFINING THE ACTION SCENE

WHAT IS AN ACTION SCENE?

At its most basic level, an action scene is an expression of plot or character development through violence.

Wait, violence? Is that really necessary?

In a word, yes. We're still essentially the same cantankerous hominids we were a hundred thousand years ago. Ever since the first proto-human got angry about something done by one of his neighbors and picked up a rock to bash the other fellow's head in, we've been solving our disagreements through violent acts. And over the millennia, we've gotten very, very good at it.

We may use the trappings of civilization to try to curb our instinctive violent cores, but in the long run, virtually anyone is capable of committing violence at some level. Because of that, action scenes in media play to our low brains. Perhaps it's some kind of Jungian racial memory, but when we observe others in action, it gives us a kind of catharsis we haven't been able to obtain socially for thousands of years. That's why an action scene has to be every bit as important and planned out as a dramatic conversation, an erotic encounter, or a beautiful description. Readers crave that kind of feeling, and it's up to you to provide it.

Can an action scene be nonviolent?

Sorry, pacifists. No, it cannot. Because action scenes are defined by some level of violence, you cannot have a nonviolent action scene. Scenes without violence are driven forward by other impetuses, such as dialogue or emotional content. Sooner or later, though, a character will choose to take action which is counter to the goals of another character, and that will beget violence.

Your best bet is to make sure it's a good scene.

WHO IS INVOLVED IN ACTION SCENES?

I've already hinted at this above. At its most basic level, an action scene involves two characters: the Hero (the narrator or focal character of the narrative) and the Opponent. The Hero is, of course, who your story is about. The Hero has a goal of some kind, and the Opponent has a goal which opposes it. That opposition creates the conflict which is the root of all action scenes (and indeed, all fiction). Without an Opponent, there can't be any conflict except the Hero's internal conflict, and that type of conflict cannot be resolved through action scenes.

When I say Opponent, I don't necessarily mean it *has* to be another character. If your Hero has to defeat a series of mechanical traps that will try to kill him before he reaches the Golden Cup of Valhalla (or whatever), those traps are Opponents; their goal is to kill him, while the Hero's goal is to survive. Opposite goals equals conflict equals action.

The problem with using non-character Opponents is that their goals can't change in response to the actions of the Hero. In the example above, if the Hero decides to forgo the traps and the Golden Cup to go party with Heidi the Valkyrie instead, the traps can't get angry and come after him. If you want real excitement and drama in your action scenes, Opponents should be characters. Let's look at the four essential types of conflict in literature and why three of them don't really work as a basis for action scenes.

Character vs. Self

This type of conflict stems from a character having a problem with him- or herself. This makes for compelling drama and loads of introspection. Unfortunately, what it doesn't lend itself to is action. Unless you're going to have your character beating himself to a pulp in a bathroom, internal conflicts just aren't resolved by the external means of action scenes. Let's let our poor, conflicted characters figure themselves out and move onward to the next kind.

Character vs. Society

At first glance, this might seem to work well for the basis of an action scene. Your character is fighting against something about his society. Doesn't that make him a rebel, prone to action? Well, no, not really. In this type of narrative conflict, the characters' issues are with social norms, mores, and other cultural factors. You can't really write a character having a fistfight with racism, for example. That's not the same as battling *agents* of society, but that's a different type of conflict.

Character vs. Nature

Now we're getting somewhere. How many movies have this as their basis? It can be very exciting, watching characters as they flee molten lava, tornadoes, earthquakes, meteors, etc. There's room for lots of spectacle and insane action as Nature pushes on its merciless course. The main issue with this type of conflict when it comes to action scenes is the fact that Nature is not only merciless, but has no antipathy toward the characters. It may seem like the avalanche is trying to kill the characters, but the fact is that forces of Nature happen whether the characters are in the way or not. Yes, it can create action, but an essential element of a true action scene is missing: the goal of the Opponent. Nature has no goals; Nature only exists. While this kind of conflict can sustain a story for awhile, eventually the reader will want to see a clear Opponent for the Hero—one whose goals work against the Hero. Overcoming Nature is possible but nowhere near as rewarding as overcoming an active Opponent.

Character vs. Other

This is the meat and potatoes of the action scene. When a character or group of characters enters into some kind of direct conflict with another character or group of characters (or machines, or zombies, or genius biker punks—you get the picture!), it becomes the catalyst for action scenes. In fact, all the other types of narrative conflict can make a story better if you can make the ultimate conflict personal: Hero versus Opponent.

Say your Hero is suffering from a mental disorder that is causing him to question his every move, paralyzing him. Okay, that's great, but if he discovers the root cause of his problem is that he was imprisoned and brainwashed by a sinister organization, he now has an identifiable Opponent, which makes his eventual victory (we hope!) much sweeter. Rebels against the Evil Empire is a noble cause, but when they're battling the Empire's top military commander, it becomes a personal conflict.

WHERE DO ACTION SCENES TAKE PLACE?

In short, anywhere you want to set them.

I call the location of an action scene the *set piece.* Set pieces are crucial aspects of any action. Take two characters who are going to fight each other. Put them in a doctor's office. Now put them on a beach. Now put them in a crosswalk. Each of those scenes has the same basic conflict: two characters fight. But the setting itself necessarily dictates their actions within that scene. Characters in action will always interact with their surrounding environment, and that can be crucial in the development and resolution of conflict. Crashing through a picture glass window in a frontier town bar is quite different from crashing though a picture glass window on the 43rd floor of a Manhattan skyscraper.

A set piece doesn't have to be a static location like a room or a battlefield. Think about car chase scenes, for example. The road itself becomes the set piece, and the characters in their vehicles move through it.

When you're creating your set piece, take a little time to populate it with objects and bystanders. You don't have to mark every single item and person in a given location, but if the Hero and Opponent are going to interact with them in some way, give them a little thought and a reason to be where they are. If you really want your Hero to use a chainsaw against the zombies, he's not going to realistically find one in the pizza joint. He will, however, find heavy pans, two-handed pizza slicers (have you ever seen one? They're *wicked!*), and cooking oil. On the other hand, any number of interesting bystanders might be in the restaurant noshing on the Triple Pepperoni Heartburn Special when the zombies come. So if you have a mean streak toward Caucasian suburban thug wannabes, and have the zombies grab one when he trips over his pants because they only go halfway up his thighs, go right ahead.

Just make sure it all makes sense, because if your action scene doesn't follow the logic of the world you've created, it will come across as fake and hollow.

WHY AN ACTION SCENE AT ALL?

Like all good fiction, it all comes down to conflict and the ways a character can choose to resolve it. Ultimately, these boil down to three possibilities. Any of these are legitimate means for dealing with the central conflict of your story, and be sure to weigh the pros and cons of each one when deciding your character's route.

Avoidance. The character chooses to avoid taking action in the face of conflict. This is the ultimate non-violent solution. This is a fairly common choice in the real world because people either don't want to get involved or else choose to involve themselves in a non-confrontational way. This is the equivalent of not answering the door when the Jehovah's Witnesses come calling.

Dialogue. The character chooses non-violent, active methods to resolve conflict. This often means the character argues his position or opens a negotiation dialogue with the opponent. This is a very common method of conflict resolution in the real world in a variety of circumstances. Dialogue is the staple tool of the courtroom drama, for example.

Action. Sometimes a problem is too serious to avoid, and the time for dialogue has passed. In those moments, an action scene must suffice. Or, as Padme Amidala described it in *Star Wars: Episode II – Attack of the Clones*, "aggressive negotiation."

EXERCISES

1. Take an action sequence from your favorite movie and break it down according to *Who*, *What*, *Where*, and *Why*.

2. Analyze camera angles and compare them to narrative focus. How does a panoramic shot of a battle compare to a closeup of a character in that battle? In a narrative, how does a global, omniscient narrator change a reader's perception of a battle from a close, limited narrator?

PART II: BUILDING BLOCKS OF ACTION SCENES

1. THE STUNT

Excerpt from Pariah's Moon by Ian Thomas Healy, Copyright 2011

Giele whipped the pan out, up, and across Rarik's face. It rang with the impact of iron on bone as Rarik flew backward into the middle of the aisle. Giele whirled around as the Dwarf shouted and fired his pistol. The bullet hit the pan with such force it almost twisted the handle from Giele's grasp. His hand went numb from the vibration of the metal. He glanced down and saw the bullet embedded in the pan's bottom. God's Blood! It had almost burst through the thick iron and into his chest.

The one-eyed Dwarf aimed again, pistol raised up toward Giele's head. He hurled the pan at the Dwarf. He tried to duck, but the iron edge caught him behind his right ear. He went down as fast as if Giele had shot him.

Giele yanked his knife from the scabbard strapped against the small of his back just as Cianid brought a jar of preserves down on the other Elf's head. His eyes rolled back and he dropped, bleeding blood and raspberries.

"Nicely done." Giele sheathed the blade again.

"Idiot. I had things under control until you got involved. Does trouble follow you everywhere or do you have to seek it out?"

The *Stunt* is the basic building block of the action scene. Think of a Stunt as a single camera shot or closely-related shots in film. All action scenes, even the most complex, can be broken down into a series of Stunts. A Stunt is either a single action undertaken by a character, or a brief flurry of related actions.

There are four Stunts in the example at the beginning of this section. They are:

> *1. Giele hits Rarik with the pan.*
>
> *2. The Dwarf fires his gun at Giele.*
>
> *3. Giele throws the pan at the Dwarf.*
>
> *4. Cianid hits the Elf with a jelly jar.*

Stunts have several qualities. They are generally brief, often lasting only a single sentence. If the Stunt has several actions relating to it, it could last as much as a paragraph, but that is the longest it should go. If you are writing a Stunt and it seems like it should be broken into more than one paragraph, you are writing multiple Stunts. Think like a director. If you would yell "Cut!" after an action to reset for the next shot, that's a completed Stunt. A Stunt can be described at its simplest in a single sentence, like the examples above: *Character does something.*

Stunts always occur within a single set piece. Characters performing Stunts don't have to stay rooted to one spot, but if they move significantly within the set piece, it's probably multiple Stunts. Because Stunts are brief in real time, there isn't much room for dialogue, lengthy description, or internal monologuing.

One of the most important aspects of a Stunt is that it and of itself will never resolve a main conflict. The equivalent would be spending two hundred pages setting everything up, only to have your Hero walk into a room, draw his pistol, and fatally shoot the main Opponent. Can that happen? Yes. Is it anticlimactic and a poor way to resolve the book? Most probably. A Stunt can be part of a larger sequence that resolves a main conflict (more on that later) but single, solitary Stunts have different uses for a plot.

A Stunt can be used as an effective means to introduce either a new character or a new subplot. These are when isolated acts (of violence, remember) have long-reaching consequences for the characters of the story. Luke Skywalker is about to be killed by a Tusken Raider on Tatooine when Ben Kenobi's arrival scares off the Sand Person. A young boy watches helpless as his parents were gunned down by a mugger in an alley. That boy grows up to become Batman. Both of these events were simple, single Stunts that led to important plot points.

Isolated Stunts can also work to develop characters further. In *Raiders of the Lost Ark*, a swordsman confronts Indiana Jones, swinging his weapon in a vicious, threatening display. Indy, in turn, pulls out his gun and shoots the man. On the surface, this is a simple, entertaining moment in an entertaining film. It's memorable, which is a key aspect of isolated Stunts both in film and in fiction. It also helps to define Indy's character better. The audience instinctively understands that he's not going to take the hard path if a simpler opportunity presents itself. Throughout the series of Indiana Jones movies, this personality trait is repeated time and time again, where Indy applies more direct methods to solving problems than working out complicated solutions.

The most important aspect of a Stunt is its inclusion in more complex series of actions within a scene, and that is what is called the Engagement.

2. THE ENGAGEMENT

Excerpt from Pariah's Moon by Ian Thomas Healy, Copyright 2011

Rarik whispered something to his one-eyed Dwarf friend Vilnius. Giele narrowed his eyes. They were plotting something. The Dwarf nodded and ran back up the street along with two of his companions. "At least now we're even, five on five," called Rarik. "But even with that drunkard mage, you're out-gunned."

Giele tightened the pull on his string. "And you're a coward, Rarik. It takes a real big man to attack a bunch of unarmed natives, kill them all, and burn their homes to the ground."

"They ain't no better than stinking animals. I gunned them down where they stood." He laughed. "Even a rutting cow's got more sense than that."

Rarik's men put their hands to their holsters like they were about to draw.

Giele felt Wioo take a step forward and knew the young Hork must be blinded by his rage. "Easy, brother," said Giele in Horkish. "Our moment will come." His blood pounded in his ears and he knew the time for battle was upon them.

"You're wrong, Rarik," said Tarvy. "The Horks are a civilized people. More so than some of the Elves on this street. You're a murderer."

Rarik held up his hand to stay his men. "Padre, I ain't got no quarrel with you. You can go. You too, Cianid. We'll settle this later, you and I. This is just between me and the marked man."

"We'll stay," called Cianid. "I'd rather stand with this Pariah than roll over and rut with the likes of you."

Rarik's face grew uglier, if such a thing was even possible, and he stepped back. The tension in the air grew palpable as the other men raised their guns. Giele's gut tightened along with his bowstring. Flames appeared at the ends of Piprel's hands. Wioo crouched down in preparation for a leap to action. Giele aimed the tip of the arrow for a spot just below Rarik's throat.

Rarik's face twisted with contempt. "Arrows and spears, sticks and magic. Don't you rutting drippers know this is the Age of the Gun?" He raised the pistol and fired it up into the air.

A steam whistle rent the air and a clanking monstrosity roared around a corner up the street. It looked like a carriage but without any horses or oxen pulling it. It belched black smoke from its boiler as it charged across the dust. One of Rarik's men sat on the driver's box and worked levers, while another managed the boiler and fed it chunks of black rock. Vilnius crouched down behind a heavy wooden shield in the front, a maniacal grin on his ugly face.

A multi-barreled rifle protruded from the vehicle's nose, and the barrels began to spin. The gun thundered and spat flame. The stink of gunpowder and ash mixed with the soot from the boiler to create a gut-twisting miasma. Giele tasted the dust kicked up from the vehicle's wheels.

Rarik dove out of the way as the horseless carriage hurtled past.

Bullets tore past Giele as he loosed his arrow, only to see it shatter against the wooden shield. Cianid fired her shotgun at Vilnius but the pellets struck the wooden shield before him. Tarvy ducked out of the line of fire and dodged into a doorway. Flame jetted from Piprel's hands, incinerated the man running the boiler, and set the rear half of the vehicle on fire. The mage's face was white with terror, but he clenched his fist with success. Then a bullet struck him in the side and he fell.

"Piprel!" Giele shouted.

Cianid was closest. "I've got him. Go!" She grabbed the mage's collar and dragged him from the line of fire.

Giele and Wioo both turned and pelted for safety, weaving as they sprinted down the street. The one-eyed Dwarf swept his gun barrels back and forth, trying to mow them down, blanketing the street in a hail of lead. Giele knew they weren't going to make it and that any moment he'd feel bullets tearing through him.

Suddenly, hope! Brokorn and Efraya hurled into the street from between Skria Woodyard's Bowyer and Fletcher and the *Goose Creek Gazette*. For once, Giele was grateful the stubborn beast had disobeyed his orders. Without missing a stride, Giele and Wioo grabbed onto their antlers and swung up onto their backs.

The Greatdeer raced up the boulevard, the steam-powered monstrosity behind them belching and churning in relentless pursuit. Giele leaned down over Brokorn's neck and urged more speed out of the giant buck. "Split up! I'll draw his fire!" Giele shouted at Wioo. The Hork hunched down and leaned over. Efraya angled hard to the left. Vilnius tracked his gunfire toward Giele, and Wioo saw his opportunity. He wheeled around on Efraya, balanced for a moment on the Greatdeer's back, and then sprang high into the air with his spear over his head.

The driver never had a chance.

Wioo came down on the driver's box. His spear punched through the driver's chest and out his back, streaked with blood and entrails. Wioo gave an ululating hoot to celebrate his success and dove off the burning vehicle.

A bullet smacked into Brokorn's haunch and his leg collapsed, spilling Giele into the dust. The carriage bore down on them. Brokorn scrambled to one side, limping from his wounded leg while Giele hurried into the stable where he'd bought his horse all those weeks ago. "Watch out!" Giele cried to the Dwarven stable girl just as the vehicle crashed into the door and blocked it with a heap of smoldering wreckage. The young Dwarf lass screamed and ran as fast as her stubby little legs would carry her. She disappeared out the rear entrance. Giele dove for cover as a bullet whistled past his head.

We've covered the Stunt as the basic building block of the Action Scene. When we take a series of Stunts grouped together in a set piece, it forms an *Engagement*. An Engagement is an action scene involving multiple Stunts, tied together to form a complete plot point. The example scene above is set along the main street of a frontier town (the set piece) and contains several distinct Stunts. If we analyze the scene in detail here's what we learn:

Set piece: The dusty, main street of a frontier town with buildings like a newspaper office, bowyer shop, and stables.

Heroes: Giele (Narrative Focus), Wioo, Cianid, Piprel, Tarvy

Opponents: Rarik, Vilnius, other unnamed men

Stunt 1: The Steam Carriage attacks

Stunt 2: Giele fires an arrow at the Steam Carriage

Stunt 3: Cianid shoots her shotgun at the Steam Carriage

Stunt 4: Tarvy retreats.

Stunt 5: Piprel uses magic against the Steam Carriage and kills one opponent, but gets shot.

Stunt 6: Giele and Wioo flee before the onrushing Steam Carriage

Stunt 7: Giele and Wioo mount their Greatdeer and are chased by the Steam Carriage.

Stunt 8: Wioo counterattacks and kills the Steam Carriage's driver.

Stunt 9: Giele's Greatdeer is shot and Giele retreats on foot into the stable.

Stunt 10: The uncontrolled Steam Carriage crashes into the stable.

Does that seem like a lot of stuff going on in just a couple of pages? Most of those Stunts are single sentences, with a few stretching into short paragraphs. Analyzing that Engagement provides the full scene breakdown. When you want to write your own Engagement, start with a scene breakdown. Don't worry if it's dry; you can dress it once you actually start the process of writing. By doing a detailed analysis like this ahead of time, you'll find it's much easier to keep the flow of action progressing in an orderly and logical way.

Order and logic are very important parts of an Engagement. You must establish a sequence of events that works within the context of the story and makes sense from a continuity standpoint. You don't want your characters to be fighting on a rooftop and suddenly have to dodge traffic, for example, because you forgot to move them to street level during the course of the scene. Actions taken by the Heroes and Opponents must be logical and consistent with the qualities of their personalities. Would a devout nun pick up an assault rifle and fire it into a crowd? Probably not… unless she's been pushed "over the edge" to take the irrevocable action of killing. Would your sniper villain charge at your hero, brandishing his gun and yelling like a lunatic? Unlikely. As you plot out the Stunts within an Engagement, be sure you take into account the cause and effect of prior actions so the scene flows.

Engagements have several important qualities, all of which should be present for the scene to work most effectively. An Engagement must contain a minimum of two distinct Stunts, each one characterized by its own specific defining points. Most Engagements contain many Stunts. The Stunts must be related to each other, using a character or group as the bridging influence from Stunt to Stunt. It's important to have the common thread running through all your Stunts in an Engagement or else the scene will lose any sense of continuity and flow.

One of the most important aspects of an Engagement is that it must take place in a single set piece, and the characters must move through that set piece in some way. As Stunts are characterized by single, brief actions, Engagements are characterized by motion within a set piece. The set piece of an Engagement doesn't have to be a static environment; a chase down a busy highway or a space battle amid a field of whirling asteroids are also suitable set pieces for Engagements.

Any number of things may start an Engagement, but it must end in one of two ways: another Engagement, or a resolution of a conflict/plot point.

Engagement leading to another Engagement

When writing an Engagement, you may find that you want to transform it from one type of action scene, such as a chase, to another, such as a fight. Engagements work well when they transform styles this way, because the transition gives you a new set piece to work with. It adds to the sense of motion and excitement in any action scene. Just realize that you can get carried away running from Engagement to Engagement to Engagement. Sooner or later you're going to have to find an end to the series, and that requires you to resolve something.

Engagement leading to a Resolution

At the end of an Engagement, a major plot point or conflict *must* be resolved. This is because an open-ended Engagement that resolves nothing is essentially just filler and should realistically be cut from the story. You may love dump truck chases and have written a fantastic dump truck chase for your story, but if there's no resolution at the end (the bad guys get caught, the heroes escape, etc.), then all you've done is write a pointless scene.

Engagement as a character development tool

One of the most useful things you can do with an Engagement is use it to strengthen character relationships. Stressful situations naturally bring people closer together, and the action scenes you create are no different. You might think that a well-paced scene would preclude character development, but in any well-crafted scene, the characters will have to relate to one another, and often this can lead to greater understanding between the characters and a greater understanding by the reader.

Finally, the Engagement forms a portion of the famed, legendary action scene known as the Sequence.

3. THE SEQUENCE

Excerpt from Pariah's Moon by Ian Thomas Healy, Copyright 2011

Nearby timbers ignited as the boiler fire spread. Giele whipped an arrow from his quiver and ducked behind a pillar. His bow appeared undamaged despite him rolling across it. He hoped it would hold together.

Vilnius leaped clear of the burning wreck, his pistol out, and ducked behind a feeding trough. The horses in the stable reared and screamed in fear of the sudden collision and flames. Behind Giele, a wide-eyed stallion began kicking at the door to his enclosure.

Giele couldn't see through the rising smoke, couldn't think with the noise of the horses. His heart pounded in his chest. Where was Vilnius? Then he saw motion and caught a glimpse of the Dwarf as he peeked out to one side of the feeding trough. Giele loosed his arrow at Vilnius. It stuck into the trough an inch from the Dwarf's face. He fired two shots at the Elf. Giele leaped across the aisle and pressed himself into a dark alcove, feeling for another arrow. His heart gave a sick lurch as he realized he had three left in his quiver—he must have lost the rest when he fell from Brokorn. Did he still have the one marked for Rarik? Relief washed over him as he felt it, still upside-down in his quiver.

The horses screamed in terror and kicked at the walls. Wood splintered somewhere behind Giele as a mare forced her way through a partition. The Dwarf glanced in her direction. In Vilnius' moment of distraction, Giele scrambled up and over a stall divider to get a little closer to him.

"Give it up, marked man." Vilnius fired two more shots. The loose horse thundered up the aisle toward Giele. She screamed and reared as a flaming crossbeam fell down by the doorway. Vilnius cursed and flung himself away from the trough as it caught fire. He fired once and the horse fell, a hole beneath one ear where the bullet struck her.

In that moment, Giele had him dead to rights, and he was going to put a shaft right through the Dwarf's eye patch. He drew the arrow back and the bow that had served him so well over the past month shattered in his hands. The string lashed across his face and splinters sliced into his hands and cheeks like razors.

"Ha!" The Dwarf leveled his pistol at Giele. "You cling to the old ways like an old fool, Pariah. Only a half-wit brings a bow to a gunfight."

Giele's eyes watered from the sting of the bowstring and the smoke in the air. He shook his head to clear his vision.

The Dwarf's cruel laughter grated in Giele's ears. "I'm going to enjoy this."

A sharp tree branch crashed through the wall behind him, and two points burst out of his chest.

One was broken.

Giele dropped to the floor as Vilnius' final bullet whizzed over his head. The Dwarf's feet left the ground as his life gurgled out. Giele saw the glare in Brokorn's eyes as he snapped his head aside and flung Vilnius' corpse with contempt. The small body landed atop the flaming crossbeam and didn't move.

Giele ran over to Brokorn. Blood ran from a wound between his antlers, making his face a gory mask. He must have charged at the wall with all the speed of a buck in rutting season. The Dwarf's blood streaked his antlers and his own blood ran down his leg from where he'd been shot.

Giele slapped the side of his neck. "Well done, my friend." Brokorn snorted in satisfaction. His fierce pride flowed through their shared bond.

"Giele!" Wioo came in the far side of the stable. His voice was tinged with panic and his eyes bulged as he searched for his blood brother through the smoke and flames.

"I'm here, Wioo. I'm fine. Help me get the horses out of here. Be careful, they're scared."

They hurried down the aisle, opening latches and throwing aside doors. The horses bucked and kicked but ran for the far stable exit away from the flames.

It was getting difficult to breathe in the thick, smoky air as fire engulfed one wall. Wioo had to shout over the roar of the fire. "You hurt?"

"No, are you?"

"Arm broken."

They both scrambled out of the stable so Giele could check Wioo's left arm, which hung at an awkward angle. His face was calm and betrayed no pain, but there was no way he could continue to fight. "Leave Rarik to me," said Giele.

Wioo didn't want to back out of the fight. Giele saw it in his face, but his Horkish practicality made him nod in agreement. "Wioo cannot fight now. Good luck, Brother."

Giele drew his pistol. "Time to end this. Once more, my friend," he told Brokorn. The Greatdeer bowed his head and let the Elf swing up onto his back. Over the crackle of flames, Giele heard the jangle of the approaching fire wagon and the shouts of those running to assist. "Get back to the parsonage," Giele said to Wioo. "It's the safest place for you now. Wait for me there."

"*Faw.*" The young Hork turned and staggered off through the smoke. Wind whipped through the town, kicking up a great cloud of dust and smoke that swirled around the buildings. The breeze was hot and stuffy and reeked of magic, like hot iron in the rain.

Giele spurred Brokorn forward and together they charged forward like a single being with but one mission. They passed by the fire wagon and several

Elves and Dwarves on horseback. Giele recognized Deputy Sheksi, who yelled something after him but Giele couldn't hear over the thundering in his ears.

Cianid and the wounded Piprel were trapped behind a fence across a vacant lot between two buildings. Giele's fury rose. Three men crouched behind a wagon, taking occasional shots to keep Cianid from moving. Piprel lay unmoving on his back, blood staining his boiler coveralls. If he still lived, he needed a doctor right away. If he didn't, it was one more death for which Rarik would have to answer. As Giele approached, one of the men charged while the other two cut loose with a withering burst of covering fire. Cianid raised her gun.

"Cianid, don't! It's a—"

Giele's warning fell upon deaf ears, for she popped up, her face blazing with courage and streaked with smoke, and delivered a shotgun blast to the advancing man's chest. A hail of bullets pounded into the fence and she ducked back.

"God's Blood!" Giele didn't know how she avoided being riddled but she appeared unharmed, to his great relief.

The two other gunmen spotted Giele and turned their pistols in his direction. He slipped backwards off Brokorn's hips and hit the ground in a forward roll as bullets whistled over his head. He turned his momentum from the roll into a dive, extending himself out to become as small a target as possible, and fired his pistol with quick, military precision. Two shots, two kills.

Where was that rutting coward Rarik?

With a crash, Tarvy and another man fell out of a nearby ground-floor window and tumbled across the wooden porch into the street. They wrestled over the man's pistol until Tarvy delivered an impressive uppercut to the man's chin. The pistol went flying to one side as they continued to roll around.

Giele took aim but didn't dare fire with Tarvy so close to the other man. "Don't shoot, Cianid!"

She reloaded her shotgun barrels and nodded.

Tarvy rolled on top of his opponent and cuffed the man across the face. The man's struggles ceased. His sides heaving, blood running from his nose, Tarvy looked down at the man and gave him a grim smile. "I'm already forgiven for this. It will take longer for you to earn God's blessing, I'm certain."

Shots rang out. Two bloody stars appeared on Tarvy's chest. For a moment, Giele didn't understand what had happened. As he toppled, Tarvy gasped, "Rarik."

Giele whirled to see Rarik astride a bay horse, a rifle raised to his cheek, pointed at him. Giele froze, caught off-guard. Cianid screamed at Rarik and fired her shotgun, but he was too far for the pellets to do more than sting. Her action galvanized Giele, and he fired a wild shot at Rarik. His first shot hit the ground near the horse's feet. Giele corrected his aim and shot again, but the animal bucked and his second bullet grazed its flank instead of hitting Rarik in the chest. He fired his rifle back at Giele. Fire burned in Giele's right shoulder, his arm went numb, and his pistol fell to the dust. Rarik wheeled his horse around and sped off to the east.

He was running for home, and reinforcements.

Giele staggered back to his feet and choked out a whistle as he picked up the pistol and shoved it back into its holster. "Breath and Bones," he hissed. "I thought being shot in the leg hurt!" Brokorn hurried up next to him. Giele yelled from the agony as he hauled himself onto Brokorn's back.

"Giele!" called Cianid.

He almost turned back, knowing she needed help. Tarvy and Piprel were wounded, maybe dying, but there was nothing Giele could do for them now, and Rarik was getting away. If he made it to the safety of his family's estate…

The scene above is a continuation of the scene at the beginning of the Engagement section. Go back and read that scene and then read this one. What you have is a complete action scene called a Sequence. A Sequence is a combination of Engagements, connected via either the same characters, same settings, or same conflict. The Sequence above contains a total of three separate Engagements, each with their own series of Stunts. In outline, it would look like this:

Engagement 1: Heroes versus the Steam Carriage

Set piece: The dusty, main street of a frontier town with buildings like a newspaper office, bowyer shop, and stables.

Heroes: Giele (Narrative Focus), Wioo, Cianid, Piprel, Tarvy

Opponents: Rarik, Vilnius, other unnamed men

Stunt 1: The Steam Carriage attacks

Stunt 2: Giele fires an arrow at the Steam Carriage

Stunt 3: Cianid shoots her shotgun at the Steam Carriage

Stunt 4: Tarvy retreats.

Stunt 5: Piprel uses magic against the Steam Carriage and kills one opponent, but gets shot.

Stunt 6: Giele and Wioo flee before the onrushing Steam Carriage

Stunt 7: Giele and Wioo mount their Greatdeer and are chased by the Steam Carriage.

Stunt 8: Wioo counterattacks and kills the Steam Carriage's driver.

Stunt 9: Giele's Greatdeer is shot and Giele retreats on foot into the stable.

Stunt 10: The uncontrolled Steam Carriage crashes into the stable.

Engagement 2: Giele versus Vilnius the dwarf

Set piece: The burning stable.

Hero: Giele (Narrative Focus)

Opponent: Vilnius

Stunt 1: Giele shoots arrow at Vilnius and misses. Vilnius shoots back and misses.

Stunt 2: Horse escapes stall, Vilnius shoots it.

Stunt 3: Giele's bow breaks.

Stunt 4: The Greatdeer gores Vilnius through the wall.

Engagement 3: Heroes versus Rarik and his men

Set piece: Same as for Engagement 1

Heroes: Same as for Engagement 1

Opponents: Same as for Engagement 1, minus Vilnius

Stunt 1: Ciele shoots an opponent and avoids being shot.

Stunt 2: Giele shoots the two men firing at Ciele.

Stunt 3: Tarvy battles an opponent in hand-to-hand combat.

Stunt 4: Rarik shoots Tarvy.

Stunt 5: Cianid and Giele shoot at Rarik, but he flees.

Stunt 6: Giele pursues Rarik.

Engagement 3 would logically lead to Engagement 4, probably a chase scene. It might resolve the conflict or possibly lead to yet another Engagement. Sooner or later, though, either Giele's going to get Rarik or Rarik is going to get away—either one makes a resolution to the conflict, although the latter would be much less satisfactory to the Hero and reader than the former!

A complete Sequence must follow a logical progression from Engagement to Engagement. You as the writer must decide what is the bridging component between them. Often, but not always, the element of commonality will be the Hero or Heroes and their Opponents. Other times, the commonality will be the Hero and set piece, but with varying Opponents. There must be a clear variation between the Engagements if you want to spread them out into a Sequence. If everything in your Engagements is the same, you haven't constructed a Sequence; you've constructed a long Engagement.

Why use a Sequence at all? For increased excitement by the readers, of course. In *Star Wars*, the heroes fight their way off of the Death Star, only to have to then escape the pursuing TIE Fighters. Either of those Engagements would be sufficient on its own, but by combining them, it creates a memorable Sequence of great excitement. There's no reason that you shouldn't strive to achieve that kind of thrilling spectacle in your own storytelling.

The most important thing to remember when creating a Sequence is that it must resolve a major plot point or conflict with its resolution. Otherwise, the Sequence is pointless fluff.

The best Sequences will incorporate multiple set pieces and multiple types of Action Scenes, which will be covered in the following section.

EXERCISES

1. Take a Sequence from your favorite movie and break it down into Engagements, then further into Stunts. How do the characters move through the Sequence? How does the Sequence enhance character relationships? What important plot point or conflict does it resolve?

2. Outline your own basic Sequence: Two Engagements, each consisting of at least five distinct Stunts. Make sure you define your Heroes, Opponents, and set pieces accordingly. Think like a director!

PART III: TYPES OF ACTION SCENES

The taxonomy of the action scene isn't nearly as complicated as one might imagine. There are in essence only four distinct categories of action scene, each defined by specific characteristics that are unique. All scenes, whether in film or on the page, fall into one of these four categories: The Fight, The Shootout, The Chase, and The Battle. In this section, we'll look at each one of these types of action scene in great detail to better understand their crucial elements.

1. THE FIGHT

or, "Two Men Enter, One Man Leaves."

A physical contest between two individuals is probably the oldest kind of conflict in human evolution, and forms the cornerstone of all action. In any violent conflict, if you strip away all the weapons, gadgetry, vehicles, costumes, etc., you're left with two naked savages trying to overpower each other with brute strength. It sounds uncivilized, because it is.

Fights can be broken down into three sub-categories: *Mano a Mano,* the *Gang-Up*, and the *Brawl.*

Mano a Mano, Spanish for hand-to-hand, represents the most basic of all action scenes: two characters fighting in close quarters. This kind of fight can be unarmed, meaning the only weapons the characters use will be their own bodies—like a martial arts duel with punching and kicking—or with melee weapons of any sort. Little John and Robin Hood dueling with quarterstaves on a log bridge is a Mano a Mano fight. So is the lightsaber battle between Darth Vader and Obi-Wan Kenobi in *Star Wars*. Characters may use shields in a melee fight. Some shields are designed for the purpose, like medieval bucklers or modern riot shields. Others may be improvised, like when a character grabs a crate to block a blow from an opponent.

When writing a Mano a Mano scene, the narrative can follow one character, either in first-person, third-person close Point of View (POV), or third-person omniscient. The main kinds of Stunts that will occur in a Mano a Mano scene are:

1. *Flurries of punches, kicks, slaps, or use of melee weapons,*
2. *Throwing opponents against, onto, or through parts of the set,*
3. *Wrestling and grappling,*
4. *Using pieces of the set as improvised weaponry, especially when no other weapons are available, and*
5. *Falling, because fighting is treacherous even on flat, solid ground, and most fights aren't going to take place in the best terrain.*

A Mano a Mano scene ends when one character dies, surrenders, or runs away. This last may lead to another kind of action scene which will be discussed later: The Chase.

The Gang-Up is similar to Mano a Mano, but instead involves one character or a small group fighting with a much larger group. In a Gang-Up, sides may be intentionally balanced for dramatic purposes, or the underdog may have weapons, abilities, or in some other way be a match for the larger force. This is most often the case in fiction because in reality, an underdog faced with a vastly superior force is going to wind up so much chum.

Narration in Gang-Ups requires careful planning to avoid *headhopping*, which is the bane of all fiction and especially the action scene. If you are using a first-person or third-person close POV, you must take extra care not to narrate things that the POV character cannot know. For example, if your hero is battling three enemy swordsmen on a staircase in a castle, he can't know that one of his allies is perched on an adjoining tower, preparing to cast a fireball spell through a window. All he'll know is that a blast of flame comes into the stairwell and incinerates the enemy soldiers. He may be able to draw a conclusion as to what happened, but he can't know for certain if the narrative is only following him. You may find an omniscient viewpoint is easier when writing a fight of this type.

Stunts in a Gang-Up will be essentially the same as those used in Mano a Mano, and the scene will end when one side dies, surrenders, or escapes.

The Brawl is the most difficult type of fight to write. It is a fight between two large groups or a free-for-all between numerous characters with no clear sides. The difficulty in constructing a Brawl in fiction is how to narrate it. Most writers automatically pull back to use a third-person omniscient narrative, but in reality, that isn't usually the best choice. The problem with third-person omniscient in this case is that there are far too many characters to keep track of. When writers try to do so, they wind up bogging down the action and interfering with the reader's association with the narrative focal characters. It also creates a "Dispassionate Distance," which makes injuries and deaths meaningless to the reader. Remember, your stories are about people (or should be), not about events. A huge fight may be a grandiose spectacle to behold, but the reader wants to know first and foremost what happens to the Hero.

When writing a Brawl, consider approaching it using a third-person close or first person narrative, and make sure you keep the focus upon what the character can see/hear/otherwise experience with his or her senses. Imagine the confusion of trying to write a bar fight with twenty different characters, four of which are the Heroes. Now approach that same scene but keep the camera on just one character. She may be aware of what's happening off to one side, but she won't see the big guy sneaking up behind her, until one of her allies clocks him with a beer mug and he hits the floor beside her.

Here are some well-known cinematic examples of different kinds of Fights. Imagine how you as a writer might try to capture the essence of each of these scenes.

Mano a Mano

1. The Bride vs. O-ren Ishi-i in *Kill Bill, Vol. 1*
2. Obi-Wan Kenobi vs. Darth Vader in *Star Wars: A New Hope*

3. Indiana Jones vs. the Big Bald Nazi Mechanic in *Raiders of the Lost Ark*

The Gang-Up

1. Neo vs. multiple Agent Smiths in *The Matrix: Reloaded*

2. The Fellowship heroes vs. the Cave Troll in *The Lord of the Rings: Fellowship of the Ring*

The Brawl

1. Soldiers vs. sailors in the bar in *1941*

2. Bouncers vs. everyone else in *Roadhouse*

EXERCISE

Write a sample fight scene, using at least five different Stunts, from beginning to end.

2. THE SHOOTOUT

or, "PEW PEW PEW!"

Once upon a time, humans developed technology that allowed us to stand away from our opponents and kill them at a distance. Ever since then, we've been obsessed with ranged combat in all its myriad forms.

In fiction, there are three rather broad categories of ranged weapons, roughly equivalent to the past, the present, and the future: arrows, bullets, and lasers. Note that these are personal hand weapons as opposed to large siege engines requiring a crew, for example; those fall under a different style of action scene which will be discussed later. *Arrows* in this circumstance refers to any kind of pre-gunpowder projectile, either thrown, slung, or launched using string tension. *Bullets* mean any projectile fired using gunpowder (or a variation thereof). *Lasers* refer to any kind of futuristic energy weapon based upon technology not yet invented.

Action scenes involving ranged combat are similar in setup to Fights. You still need to work out the details of the set piece and where your characters fit within that area. The primary difference between a Shootout and a Fight is the distance between the opponents. No matter what type of weapon in use during a Shootout, the goal of each character should be the same: *Shoot your opponent before your opponent shoots you.*

Stunts in Shootouts will generally fall under the following categories:

> *1. Shooting your weapon at your opponent.*
>
> *2. Moving through fire between cover to close or increase the distance between you and your opponent.*
>
> *3. Using the set piece to your advantage, ie: taking cover, moving to high ground, or shooting set piece elements to change the outcome of the shootout. Example: firing an arrow through a rope supporting a heavy cask which then falls upon your opponent, catching him unawares.*

Narrating a Shootout works best in either first-person or third-person close. If you're beginning to detect a pattern here in using limited points-of-view for action scenes, you're right. The further apart characters get in physical distance, the harder it is to provide effective narration from an omniscient point of view.

A Shootout ends when one side dies, surrenders, or escapes.

There are some factors in Shootouts which an author needs to pay more attention to than in a simple Fight. The first of these is *Cover. Cover* is a portion of the set piece behind which a character can hide to make it harder to hit him or her with a ranged weapon. It is the single most important factor for any character in a Shootout. If you can't see your opponent, you can't shoot him. Cover protects characters from enemy fire. It gives them a place to plan their next moves, which is something an author should take full advantage of when writing the scene. It also gives them a place to pop up/out from to fire their own weapons. Cover may be static set pieces, like wall corners, tree trunks, car doors (although a staple of cop shows and movies, not recommended because bullets go right through them), rocks, etc. They may also be mobile pieces, such as animals, vehicles, or the ever-popular human shield. In the event a character is using a mobile set piece for cover, he or she will have to move with it, or guide it if possible.

Another important factor in a Shootout is ammunition. Although you don't need to keep track of every arrow and shot fired in every situation, there will be times where that becomes important and you need to know when your character either has to reload or is out of ammunition, necessitating a change of plans. If you, the author, want to have your characters run out of ammunition at a crucial part of a scene, make sure they fire enough arrows/bullets/lasers beforehand. A soldier in a pitched battle in World War II, for example, has access to a great many rounds of ammunition, either his own or from fallen comrades. The same soldier who's parachuted down behind enemy lines may only have six bullets with which to fight his way back to his allies. Reloading a weapon is always a good opportunity for characters to interact with other characters, whether whispering to each other behind cover about their next move or shouting across open space to taunt opponents.

Wounds are a big factor of any action scene, but they have a special place in the Shootout. Injuries that happen in the course of a Fight often have their effects minimized until after the engagement because of adrenaline, guts, or whatever the fiction equivalent is in your world. In a Shootout, wounds are much more immediate, often painful and possibly quite damaging. The character is under high stress from being in a combat situation, but if he is behind cover and takes a bullet, he will have much more time to realize how much it hurts and how badly he may have been wounded. Because of the penetrating nature of ranged projectiles, victims in Shootouts may find themselves peppered with buckshot, grazed by bullets, pierced by arrows or spears, or burned and charred by lasers or blasters. As a writer, it is imperative to take full advantage of those opportunities to make your characters more believable and bring the readers closer to them.

Here are some well-known cinematic examples of different Shootouts. Imagine how you as a writer might try to capture the essence of each of these scenes.

1. El Mariachi versus the bar thugs in *Desperado.*

2. Luke and Leia versus the Stormtroopers over the Death Star shaft in *Star Wars: The Empire Strikes Back.*

3. Robin Hood's men versus the Sheriff's men in *Robin Hood: Prince of Thieves.*

EXERCISE

Write a sample Shootout scene, using at least five different Stunts, from beginning to end. Pay special attention to Cover, Ammunition, and Wounds.

3. THE CHASE

or, "We're about to enter Hot Pursuit!"

There's something very primal about a chase scene. It goes all the way back to when humans were still hunter-gatherers and before. We revel in the thrill of the chase, whether it's from the perspective of the hunter chasing after the prey or from the perspective of the fugitive fleeing before the predator. Either type of scenario gets our blood flowing and witnessing one on film or reading one in a book can have the same kind of cathartic response. The essence of a chase scene is very simple: one character is trying to escape from another. What makes a scene exciting is how that escape attempt happens and whether or not it is successful.

All chase scenes boil down into one of two varieties: the chase can be on foot, or it can be in vehicles.

For a chase scene *on foot*, your Hero can either be the pursuer or the escapee. Weapons may be utilized during a chase scene on foot, but remember that certain weapons are ineffective to use while running, such as two-handed swords, crossbows, man-portable rocket launchers, etc. A more likely scenario is that the use of weapons will be suspended during the chase and brought to bear if the chase ends by the pursuer catching the potential escapee.

When writing a chase scene, remember that it cannot be a single Stunt. A chase is always an Engagement, with the characters moving through a set piece or series of set pieces. It's useful to plan the route your characters will take ahead of time, taking care to note any points along the path which present an opportunity for specific stunts or interactions.

Chase scenes can be written in first-person point-of-view, third-person close, or third-person omniscient. This last affords the writer the opportunity to narrate stunts and interactions from perspectives of both the pursuer and the pursued, although it's imperative to avoid head-hopping.

Typical Stunts that occur during a chase scene on foot include the following:

> *1. Running, jumping, falling, and climbing through portions of the set piece.*
>
> *2. Crashing through solid or apparently-solid parts of the set piece such as walls, doors, windows, floors, and ceilings.*
>
> *3. Knocking set pieces in the way of the pursuer. Think of a typical foot chase scene in a movie. The characters probably run through a hotel kitchen at some point, and there's always a handy rack of trays or hapless waiter to pull down, presenting an obstacle to the pursuer.*
>
> *4. Firing ranged weapons if possible. Often, this means either the pursuer or pursued has to stop momentarily to fire/shoot/throw a weapon.*
>
> *5. Avoiding dangerous parts of the set pieces such as moving cars, low-flying air-speeders, robotic factory equipment, or any number of traps.*

Chase scenes *in vehicles* offer the greatly-increased thrill factor of speed. Olympic gold medalist Usain Bolt topped out at about 27.5 miles per hour at his world record sprint, but that's nothing compared to a high-speed chase down a highway at speeds over a hundred miles per hour, or space opera chases a hundred times faster than that. Even a chase on horseback adds that additional thrill of greater speed (for these purposes, anything the characters are riding counts as a vehicle, even if it's a creature).

Characters in vehicular chase scenes may be drivers/pilots or passengers. Each has advantages and disadvantages. A driver/pilot must give a significant portion of his or her attention over to guiding the vehicle, which limits the activities that can be performed. A passenger has much more leeway to act independently, but has no direct control over the speed, orientation, and direction of the vehicle.

Combat is more likely to occur between characters in a vehicular chase than in one on foot. This is because although vehicle operation may be strenuous and stressful, the characters don't generally also have to devote attention to keeping their feet moving as well. There are two types of combat involving vehicles:

> *1. Using weapons, either mounted on the vehicle (such as a tank's gun or the laser cannons on a starfighter) or handheld by passengers (like the prototypical '70s cop hanging his pistol out the window to*

> *shoot at somebody's tires). Related to this is the Fight which takes place on board a moving vehicle, such as a cowboy wrestling with a Sioux warrior over a knife on the roof of a stagecoach.*
>
> *2. Using the vehicle itself as a weapon (such as intentional collisions or running an opponent off the road), which is more common in settings where vehicular weapons aren't common.*

Narration for vehicular chase scenes works best in first-person or third-person close point of view. Third-person omniscient can be used, but it becomes exponentially more difficult to keep track of numerous characters and vehicles.

Stunts in vehicular chase scenes may include:

> *1. Collisions/Ramming (of other vehicles or set pieces which may or may not shatter to permit passage).*
>
> *2. Jumping (cars, motorcycles, boats, horses, etc.), Flying actions (planes, helicopters, spaceships, dragons, etc.)*
>
> *3. Firing weapons and taking fire from opponents.*
>
> *4. Characters transferring from vehicle to vehicle, which generally leads to a Fight. Note: a Fight taking place under these circumstances does not mean the Chase has stopped. It's an Engagement within another Engagement. High-level stuff. Go for it.*
>
> *5. Avoidance of set pieces, either moving (pedestrians, other vehicles, etc.) or non-moving (fruit stands, towers, bridge abutments).*

A chase scene will end when one side is dead, surrenders, or is caught, which may then lead to a Fight and continuation into a new Engagement (thus creating a complete Sequence).

Things to take into account when writing a chase scene:

Who's Chasing Who? If the characters are the ones being chased, their goal is simple: escape. If the characters are the pursuers, their goals may be more widespread. Their objective may be to destroy those escaping—the easiest method; to stop (but not necessarily destroy) them from escaping—more difficult, and it requires the opponents to be blocked or disabled; or to capture those escaping—most difficult of all, because the opponents have to not only be blocked or disabled, but each one must be recaptured without too much injury.

Collateral Damage. Chase scenes realistically do enormous amounts of collateral damage to set pieces, bystanders, etc. For writers interested in creating lots of realism, there should be lasting consequences for characters involved in this type of sequence, and it may affect the plot.

Here are some well-known cinematic examples of different kinds of Chases. Imagine how you as a writer might try to capture the essence of each of these scenes.

Foot Chases

1. The opening sequence to *Casino Royale* (2006 version)
2. The tremendous parkour chases in *District B13*
3. Most Jackie Chan films; one of the best is in *Mr. Nice Guy*.

Vehicular Chases

1. The horseback guards chasing the wagon in *Willow*
2. The amazing freeway sequence in *The Matrix: Reloaded*
3. The TIE fighters chasing the *Millenium Falcon* through the asteroid belt in *Star Wars: The Empire Strikes Back.*
4. Pretty much every James Bond film.

EXERCISE

Write a sample Chase scene, using at least five different Stunts, from beginning to end. Pay special attention to set pieces, character actions during the chase, and speed.

4. THE BATTLE

or, "War is Hell!"

The Battle is, in my opinion, the hardest type of action scene to write *well.* When you have to manage huge groups of people, of which your characters are a part, it's a tricky process to keep them from getting lost amid all the action.

Dealing with large-scale combat requires a lot of planning on an author's part. Most authors want their hero or heroes to be instrumental parts of the battle. That means they must be involved in whatever group is performing the penultimate act. For example: your heroes may be a unit of soldiers in World War II who have to destroy a German machine gun nest so the emergency supplies can advance. There may be several units involved in the combat, but the author needs to focus on what the heroes are doing.

When planning your battle sequence, after you've divided up your armies into groups and missions, determine what the important plot points in the battle are. If you need certain events to happen at certain times, plug them into your battle timeline and write from point to point, keeping the flow of action centered on your heroes.

Do not try to describe every single Stunt in a full-scale battle. By creating a battle, you've already established there is a tremendous amount of action going on all around the characters, and the readers don't need to be told what Soldier #38 is doing when he's a thousand feet away from the heroes. If what he's doing is vitally important to the plot, you should have one of your heroes do it instead.

It's easy to get caught up in the grand, sweeping events of combat and lose your characters. Think of it as the difference between a wide-angle panoramic camera shot and a closeup in film. The panoramic shot shows everything happening, but details get lost. You may see great blasts of magic razing down troops, siege engines moving along the ground, buildings shattering. But where are your characters? Which of those tiny figures running around are the ones you've been writing about? Remember, your story is still about people, not events, and if you succumb to the temptation to show off the scale of your epic battles without tempering them with closeup shots, you will lose your reader's interest. On the other hand, if you stick solely with closeup camera angles, keeping the narrative focused only on the heroes, you may lose the sense of scale. Try to strike a good balance between them, say panoramic shots used early to establish the scene, and then lots of closeups on the heroes afterward.

Things happen in a battle which are independent of the heroes' actions. Some of these things may be the result of their actions, and some may change their actions. In the example above of the World War II unit, their destruction of the machine gun nest will allow supply units to start crossing a bridge, but now they'll be expected to provide covering fire. On the other hand, German tanks may roll in at that moment and the machine gun nest isn't the strategic point that it had been. Make sure your heroes adapt to the changing circumstances in a battle. Remember that the things which happen elsewhere in a battle may have important or disastrous effects on your heroes, even if they don't directly witness them.

Here are some examples of excellent battle scenes in film:

1. The Japanese attacking the U.S. Forces in *Pearl Harbor.*
2. Rebels and Ewoks battling Imperial troops in *Star Wars: Return of the Jedi.* Yub yub!
3. The *Star Trek: The Next Generation* episode "The Best of Both Worlds (Part 2)" where a fleet of starships battle a Borg cube ship.
4. The battle of Helm's Deep in *The Lord of the Rings: The Two Towers*

EXERCISE

Write a sample Battle scene. Create your setting, divide your armies up into units, and place your hero or heroes into one unit. Begin with a panoramic scene description and as the action starts to flow, pull the camera in on your hero and follow him or her through the battle. Make sure he or she has a specific mission to fulfill that will affect the battle's outcome.

PART IV: GRATUITOUS EXPLOSIONS AND OTHER ACTION DOWNFALLS

Writing action scenes can be a tremendous amount of fun. Your characters can do all those stunts you've seen in movies, and you can invent entirely new predicaments for them. You have to be careful not to get too carried away with that fun, because it can result in some pitfalls that can ruin even the best-planned action scene.

QUICK CUTS

This is a common problem when writers are trying to pull back and write from a "global" perspective. It's easy to do because you, the writer, can see everything that's going on in an action scene, and it's tempting to write every bit of it, because that's what writers do. Jumping around in a scene quickly, sometimes with as little as a single sentence devoted to one character followed by a sentence for another and so on, is the literary equivalent of the *jump cut* in cinema. Some directors have no sense of flow when it comes to an action scene, and they figure the frenetic camera cuts with shots lasting less than a second are a suitable equivalent.

Hint: they're not.

Jumping around in your scene from character to character, like you're trying to make sure everybody gets equal coverage, will make your scene choppy and have no flow to it. This in turn eliminates the possibility of one of the most useful aspects of action scenes: character development. As described in Part

1, an action scene can be an excellent vehicle for readers to learn more about the characters. If the scene has no flow to it because of quick cuts, this is an impossibility.

HEADHOPPING

This is generally a no-no in all types of fiction. Headhopping is when the narrative has been focusing on a single character's thoughts, words, and deeds, and suddenly in the middle of the scene the narrative switches to someone else's focus without any obvious scene break. The equivalent might be if you're playing a first-person-shooter video game and all of a sudden you're a different character. Does that sound a bit jarring? Because in fiction it's just as jarring, and in an action scene it effectively interrupts the flow as the reader has to figure out what just happened.

PURPLE PROSE

We're all writers, and we love words. It can be tempting to reach into one's thesaurus to come up with beautiful and unusual words to perfectly capture the essence of our intent. Unfortunately, there's no place for this in an action scene. Overwriting drags the pace of a scene down to a crawl as the reader has to try to follow the flow of action through a muddle of rich language. Along the same lines is the problem of the odd word choice. You may love the word *conflagration*, but a typical reader may not know it also means *fire*. I'm not saying don't use rich language at all, but if a reader doesn't know a word, it's like hitting a roadblock as they look at it, go "Huh?" and have to deduce its meaning from the language around it.

ACTION WITHOUT REACTION OR CONSEQUENCE

In reality, if you get shot (and I hope you never do!), you'll probably scream, piss yourself, vomit, go into shock, faint, or all of the above. On the other hand, heroes always seem to shrug off "minor flesh wounds," tear off a strip of their shirt to bind them, and keep on going. This is what makes our heroes exciting: the ability to battle through pain that would reduce the rest of us to quivering piles of jelly on the floor. If your hero can be shot a dozen times and be fine later in the book, then what's the point of her having been shot at all? Don't forget the lasting consequences of wounds or injuries just because the action scene is finished.

Along the same lines, don't forget that those chase scenes may leave dozens of innocent bystanders injured or killed, and cause thousands of dollars' worth of property damage. Stray bullets from a gunfight can travel a long distance. If there's no risk of consequence to the heroes, there's no need for them to act like heroes. They can blow stuff up willy-nilly, which may be cool for the first five minutes, but will get boring and unrealistic quickly.

NO RESOLUTION

Finally, it's important to remember that any Engagement or Sequence that fails to resolve even a minor plot point is completely gratuitous. A Sequence ought to resolve something *major.* If you have an idea for a car chase involving dump trucks and a drawbridge doesn't mean you should put it in your book just because it *looks cool.* If nothing has changed for the plot between the moment the heroes climb into that dump truck and the moment the truck crashes to relative safety on the other side of the open drawbridge, you're guilty of a Gratuitous Explosion. It doesn't matter if it's not an explosion. You know what I mean.

PART V: PUTTING IT ALL TOGETHER

Here's a sample outline of a complete action Sequence, including Stunts and Engagements. When you get to the part that says *Action!*, that's your cue to use this outline to write up a practice scene. This scene is set in a typical 1970s gritty rogue cop story. A blank version of this worksheet can be downloaded from http://www.writebetteraction.com.

SAMPLE ENGAGEMENT:

DETECTIVE JAMES "BIG JIM" POSTLETHWAITE

Set-up

Type of Engagement:

Fight

Source of conflict:

Mobsters want to scare off Big Jim.

Setting:

Time of day or night: Afternoon

Indoors/outdoors/weather: Underground parking garage

Bystanders:

None

Physical terrain:

Concrete, parked cars, overhead fluorescent lights

Important items in the set piece:

Fire extinguisher

Characters:

Who: Big Jim, three mobsters

Protagonist's goal:

Big Jim wants to survive the encounter and then apprehend/question the mobsters

Antagonist's goal:

Mobsters want to kill Big Jim then get away.

Equipment for each character:

- Big Jim has his service pistol and a wicked awesome mustache

- Two of the mobsters have a pistol, one has a switchblade.

Stunts:

1. Mobsters grab Big Jim as he exits the elevator and throw him against the wall.

2. As Mobster 1 takes Big Jim's pistol, Big Jim elbows him in the face.

3. Mobster 2 fires at Big Jim but misses.

4. Big Jim grabs fire extinguisher from the wall and sprays it at Mobster 2, who ducks.

5. Mobster 1 fires at Big Jim but misses.

6. Big Jim hits Mobster 1 in the face with the fire extinguisher, knocking him out.

7. Mobsters 2 and 3 turn to run as Big Jim retrieves his pistol

Action!

SAMPLE ENGAGEMENT (USING PREVIOUS STUNT)

Set-up

Type of Stunts:

- Fight

- Shootout

Source of conflict:

Big Jim vs. the Mobsters

Setting:

Time of day or night: Afternoon

Indoors/outdoors/weather: Underground parking garage

Bystanders:

None

Physical terrain:

Concrete, parked cars, overhead fluorescent lights

Important items in the set piece:

Fire extinguisher

Characters:

Who: Big Jim, three mobsters

Protagonist's goal:

Big Jim wants to survive the encounter and then apprehend/question the mobsters

Antagonist's goal:

Mobsters want to kill Big Jim then get away.

Equipment for each character:

- Big Jim has his service pistol and a wicked awesome mustache

- Two of the mobsters have a pistol, one has a switchblade.

Stunts:

1. Mobsters 2 and 3 duck behind a car for cover.

2. Mobster 2 shoots at Big Jim, who dives between two parked cars.

3. Big Jim shoots underneath the cars and hits Mobster 3 in the foot.

4. Mobster 2 runs across open space, firing blindly and almost hitting Big Jim.

5. Big Jim shoots back, breaking a car window but missing Mobster 2.

6. Mobster 2 jumps into his car and starts it.

7. As Big Jim runs out into the open part of the garage, Mobster 2 tries to run him down.

8. Big Jim shoots at the car, hitting the windshield but not Mobster 2, and then dives clear.

Action!

SAMPLE SEQUENCE (USING PREVIOUS ENGAGEMENTS)

Set-up

First Engagement: Fight

Second Engagement: Shootout

Third Engagement: Chase *(Outline this yourself)*

Fourth Engagement: Fight *(Outline this yourself)*

Action!

I would love to see how you write out these scenes. Feel free to submit them to be posted on *writebetteraction.com.* Time permitting, I will critique all submitted action scenes from this or any other project for which you're seeking feedback.

PART VI: TIPS AND TRICKS

Here are a few last minute suggestions for you to help improve your action scenes.

MAPPING TECHNIQUES

Drawing maps can be very useful when blocking out an action scene. You don't need to be Picasso or Van Gogh to do this. A simple rectangle can suffice as a room, with boxes inside it to mark furniture or other objects. Use initials for your characters and arrows to track their movements. Sometimes if you're stuck for ideas on how to write a part of an action scene, a map can be a lifesaver, because it gives you a visual representation of what is in your characters' environment and may point to methods of resolution, such as Big Jim grabbing the fire extinguisher by the elevator and using it to disable one of the Mobsters in the sample from Part 5. Using a dry-erase board, chalkboard, or even a simple graphics program can help you see step by step how your characters move through the scene.

PACING

Action scene vocabulary is much more than just the words you choose. *Pacing* is the most important part of writing your scene, and that comes down to a few sneaky techniques that most readers won't even realize you're using. It may sound contrary to logic, but the truth is that readers read longer sentences with multiple clauses *faster* than short sentences. The reason for this is simple: a reader pauses at the end of every sentence, even just for a fraction of a second. The easiest way to understand this is to read something out loud. Read this entire paragraph out loud. Which parts go slower? Which go faster?

I'd bet the first part of the preceding paragraph seemed faster, because the longer sentences read faster. The final three sentences slowed the pacing down because they're shorter and you most likely paused after the periods and question marks. When you're writing action, you'll find that a longer sentence is better for describing an action and a shorter sentence is useful for highlighting an important moment in the scene you want to stand out. For example:

> Big Jim rounded the corner at full speed, his lungs burning from too many cigarettes. The mobster was pelting down the alley, still clutching his pistol in one hand. The mobster flung a trash can into Big Jim's path, but the police officer hurdled it like he was still in the Academy. The alley turned, and ended in a brick wall. The mobster skidded to a halt, turned, and raised his pistol. Big Jim's pistol came up faster and pulled the trigger. The cylinder went *click*. Uh oh, thought Jim. No more bullets.

Did you get the sense of frantic motion in the first part of that scene? The longer sentences will feel faster to readers and then the pacing slows dramatically towards the end with those three short sentences at the end. Each one is an important moment, and the short sentence ensures that the reader won't rush through them.

VOCABULARY

Punch is a simple, common word that everyone understands. *Thesaurus.com* lists thirty-six different synonyms for the same word, none of which would be unfamiliar to the average reader. Your characters don't have to simply *punch* an opponent over and over again. They can *bash*, *jab*, *pummel*, *slug*, *smash*, and *wallop* them too. The simplest way of defining combat is hitting/shooting people until they stop moving. But the simplicity of that doesn't mean you have to limit your vocabulary. Most combat-oriented words tend to be short and familiar and because we're a bunch of cantankerous hominids, we have a lot of different words we can use.

When would you want to use longer, fancier words in an action scene? When you're writing a dramatic moment and you want to slow the pacing down, it's a good time to break them out. Imagine the parts of an action scene that might be shot in slow motion—parts where the director wants you to have time to see everything that happens. You can duplicate that feel in your writing by slowing the pacing down with longer words and shorter sentences.

ROLE-PLAYING GAMES

Yes, I know, there's a stigma associated with things like *Dungeons & Dragons*, but it doesn't change the fact that the people who have written these game systems have put in many, many hours into research and development to make them playable and fun. Working with a group of players in a tabletop RPG can fulfill a few needs of a writer. First of all, it gets us out of the house and socializing with others, which can be a challenge when we spend so much time with butt-in-chair writing. More importantly, most RPGs are centered around action and conflict resolution. There will be many chances for combat in a RPG session, and that combat may be detailed, and can include miniature figures and maps. From a writer's standpoint, it's like having the work of plotting an action scene done for you. Other players may provide actions and solutions you may not have thought of, and that in turn will expand your action vocabulary and give you a bigger toolbox.

Finally, Role-Playing Game books are often chock full of detailed information on equipment, weapons, vehicles, etc. They have often been meticulously researched by those who produce the game manuals. They can be valuable resources for writers when outfitting characters and worldbuilding.

A FINAL WORD

Thanks for reading this manual. I hope you've found some useful information in it and know a little more about how to write a good action scene. I'd love to know how you're doing with it, so feel free to visit **www.writebetteraction.com** and drop me a line. And finally, if you liked the excerpts of my own writing that I posted from *Pariah's Moon*, it's available for sale, along with many other short stories and novels, from Local Hero Press and all major ebook retailers.

GLOSSARY

ACTION SCENE – An expression of plot or character development through violence.

AMMUNITION – However many shots a character with a ranged weapon has at his or her disposal.

BLOCKING AND STAGING – The motions a character performs during the course of the scene and in what order.

BRAWL – A fight between two large groups or a free-for-all.

CHASE – An action scene where one character is trying to escape from another.

CHOREOGRAPHING – The planning of specific stunts performed by the characters in your scene.

COVER – A portion of the set piece behind which a character can hide to make it harder to hit him or her with a ranged weapon.

ENGAGEMENT – A grouping of Stunts in a single set piece, tied together to form a complete plot point.

FIGHT – An action scene involving characters using no weapons or melee weapons only.

GANG-UP – A fight between a small group and a large group.

HERO – The narrator or focal character of the narrative.

MANO A MANO – The most basic action scene, a fight between two characters in close quarters.

MELEE WEAPON – Any weapon which is used in close combat; may be a blunt smashing weapon, a bladed cutting weapon, or a sharpened piercing weapon.

NARRATIVE FOCUS – The Point-of-View character in a scene with several other characters.

OPPONENT – The character or thing that creates the conflict which is the root of all action scenes (and indeed, all fiction).

POINT OF VIEW – The kind of narration used by the writer, most often first-person or third-person (either close to one character or omniscient).

RANGED WEAPON – Any weapon designed to operate at a distance; includes arrows/spears, guns, lasers, or variations.

SCRIPTING – The dialogue of the characters uttered during an action scene.

SEQUENCE – A combination of Engagements, connected via either the same characters, same settings, or same conflict.

SET PIECE – The location where an action scene takes place.

SHIELD – Any object used to block or deflect an incoming attack; may be designed for the purpose or improvised.

SHOOTOUT – An action scene involving the use of ranged weapons.

STUNT – The basic building block of an action scene.

MORE BOOKS BY IAN THOMAS HEALY

Novels

Blood on the Ice

Hope and Undead Elvis

Pariah's Moon

Troubleshooters: The Longest Joke Ever told

The Milkman: SuperSekrit Extra Cheesy Edition

Just Cause (from New Babel Books*)*

Short Stories

Just Cause Universe series

Graceful Blur

The Scent of Rose Petals

The Steel Soldier's Gambit

Professional MotorCombat series

Last Year's Hero

Rookie Sensation

Harry Blaine series

Bulletproof

Young Guns

Tuesday Night at Powerman's

Standalone titles

In His Majesty's Postal Service

Bread and Circuses

Footprints in the Butter

Upon A Midnight Clear

Dental Plan

Collections

Tales of the Weird Wild West, Vol. 1

The Bulletproof Badge

Titles available at Local Hero Press (localheropress.ianthealy.com), Amazon.com, BarnesandNoble.com, and other online retailers.

ABOUT THE AUTHOR

Ian Thomas Healy dabbles in many different genres. His superhero novel *Deep Six: A Just Cause Novel* was a Top 100 Semi-finalist in the 2008 Amazon.com Breakthrough Novel Award. He's an eight-time participant and winner of National Novel Writing Month where he's tackled such diverse subjects as sentient alien farts, competitive forklift racing, a religion-powered rabbit-themed superhero, cyberpunk mercenaries, cowboy elves, and an unlikely combination of vampires with minor league hockey. He is also the creator of the *Writing Better Action Through Cinematic Techniques* workshop, which helps writers to improve their action scenes.

His goal is to become as integral to the genre of superhero fiction as William Gibson was to cyberpunk and Anne Rice was to urban fantasy.

When not writing, which is rare, he enjoys watching hockey, reading comic books (and serious books, too), and living in the great state of Colorado, which he shares with his wife, children, house-pets, and approximately five million other people.

Ian is on Twitter as @ianthealy

Ian is on Facebook as Author Ian Thomas Healy

www.ianthealy.com

16541972R00036

Made in the USA
San Bernardino, CA
07 November 2014